CUS—P

Mary Anne Butler

CURRENCY PRESS
The performing arts publisher

CURRENT THEATRE SERIES

First published in 2020
by Currency Press Pty Ltd,
PO Box 2287, Strawberry Hills, NSW, 2012, Australia
enquiries@currency.com.au
www.currency.com.au

in association with ATYP

Reprinted 2020.

Typeset by Dean Nottle for Currency Press.
Printed by Fineline Print + Copy Services, Revesby, NSW.
Cover image by Luke Stambouliah, art direction by Justin Stambouliah. Cover shows Jordan Dulieu.

A catalogue record for this book is available from the National Library of Australia

Contents

PLAYWRIGHT'S NOTE

Cusp started with a phone call from Fraser Corfield and Jenny Medway at ATYP, who wanted to generate a new work for young people, set in the Northern Territory.

That got me thinking about the specific issues that our young NT folk face: the things unique to living up here, as well as those which may be universal to young people across this country. In my era, there was a sort of happy complacency surrounding me: a sense that everything would somehow 'work out' in the end. I'm of the generation where university education was free (thank you, Gough) and a job was pretty much guaranteed—even for a mediocre Bachelor of Arts student such as myself.

Speaking to young people while researching *Cusp*, it increasingly struck me that the younger generations have been duped. Education is expensive, ruling out entire demographics who simply can't afford to spend three or more years studying, as opposed to going straight to work. University fees are exorbitant. Jobs are scarcer and offered under increasingly tenuous conditions. The planet they're inheriting has basically been broken by the generations before them, and they're privy to a swag of 'leadership' choices which ensure the planet continues to be further broken: by mining, fracking, ignorance and arrogance. So many life choices have been stripped from emerging generations, and I find that heartbreaking. As Elvis says in *Cusp*, 'Some people just get better choices than others'. And indeed they do.

Cusp is about three young people on the cusp of adulthood, each facing major choices which will determine their paths forward for the rest of their lives. One faces life as a single parent, another has to choose between staying fully connected to Country and community or going 'down south' to study a university course which isn't available in the NT, and a third has to change his habitual behaviour in every way, to avoid returning to prison. The stakes are high for each of them, as are the levels of resilience they have to draw on in order to overcome the obstacles which stand in the way of them living the best lives they can possibly imagine.

Given your lot in life, how *do* you make the most of what you've been dealt with? How do you make massive life decisions without the added agendas of the adults around you? How do you explore all your options if you don't even know what they are? Are you living the life you really want to live? How do you even know what that life might look like? How do you access options if you can't even see what they look like?

The writing, development and production of *Cusp* have been a beautiful ride for me: from initial commissioning by ATYP, through the two developments—one in Darwin engaging Darwin actors, and one in Sydney with Sydney-based actors—all steered beautifully by director Fraser Corfield. Input from dramaturg Jane Fitzgerald and cultural consultant Rosealee Grimes (who's based in the remote community of Yirrkala, where the character of Rosie lives) were pivotal in shaping the work, and once again I'm grateful to the generosity of the theatre folk around me who so openly give of their craft and intelligence to help forge new works into shape. *Cusp* has benefitted enormously from these collaborators.

Fraser auditioned the cast and collaborated with the all-NT design team from his Sydney base, proving that the inclusion of regional works and regionally based creatives is literally a Zoom or Skype away. ATYP and Darwin's Brown's Mart Theatre collaborated on the 2019 premiere of *Cusp* in Darwin, with a move to Griffin Theatre as part of ATYP's 2020 season. This provided an opportunity for two incredible young NT actors—musician Stevie Jean and Larrakia woman Nyasha Ogden—plus the wonderfully talented design team of Cj Fraser-Bell (set), Jessie Davis (lighting) and Brad Fawcett (sound) to showcase their work nationally. This is vital for regional practitioners—particularly young and emerging ones—and they all held their own on the premiere production with a sharpness of skill and intelligence that makes me proud to know them. Josh McElroy as the 'southern actor' moved up to Darwin for rehearsals, and I doubt this town will ever be quite the same. He was awesome, in every way.

For myself as a playwright, I get to see two completely different responses to the work within a short space of time. From my adopted hometown of Darwin (100,000 pax) to the Kings Cross centre of Sydney (5.23 million pax), it'll be interesting to see how the work translates.

There's always a whisper of hope at the end of my plays—because I believe there's always a whisper of hope in the air, somewhere. You just have to search hard for it at times. I hope young and old see themselves in *Cusp*: that audience and readers take away the elements of hope which are entrenched in the text. I hope that the more fragile amongst us feel more safely held, and more resilient after seeing or reading it, and that maybe people reach out to each other without judgment or hidden agendas once they've absorbed the essence of the work: that we're all the same, in the end. It's just that some people do get better choices to choose from. I also hope that audiences emerge feeling more empowered to make their own choices with what they've got, rather than wishing for something they don't yet have.

That's a lot of hopes for a work, I know. But there it is.

If *Cusp* was a song, it would be Chumbawamba's 'Tubthumping'. People who get knocked down, yet still manage get up again, somehow.

Cusp is a love letter to the people and landscape of Australia's Top End: in particular our youth, who hold the future so delicately and respectfully in their more-than-capable hands.

I hope you enjoy the ride.

Mary Anne Butler
February 2020

For my nieces and nephew
Tess Wilson, Alex Wilson, Sara Anne Butler and Kate Butler
May the world give you beautiful choices, and may you carve much joy out of them, in return.

Cusp was first produced by Brown's Mart Theatre and ATYP at Brown's Mart Theatre, Darwin, on 22 October 2020, with the following cast:

MADDIE	Stevie Jean
ELVIS	Josh McElroy
ROSIE	Nyasha Ogden

Director, Fraser Corfield
Dramaturg, Jane FitzGerald
Set Designer, Cj Fraser-Bell
Lighting Designer, Jessie Davis
Sound Designer and Production Manager, Brad Fawcett
Sound Design Mentor, Matt Cunliffe
Stage Manager, Scott Gooding
Cultural Consultant, Rosealee Pearson

CHARACTERS

ROSIE, 18 years old, an Indigenous Australian living in Yirrkala

ELVIS, 17 years old (cross-cultural casting encouraged)

MADDIE, 16 years old (cross-cultural casting encouraged)

SETTINGS

Shady Beach, Yirrkala (a remote Northern Australian Indigenous community)

Dondale Youth Detention Centre (Darwin)

A house in Palmerston (Darwin)

The Arnhem Club in Nhulunbuy (a remote Northern Australian Indigenous township)

The Central Arnhem Highway

Darwin Hospital

The set is minimal, and set changes are seamless segues.

This play went to press before the end of rehearsals and may differ from the play as performed.

Shady Beach, Yirrkala.

ROSIE: I love it out here. Edge of the ocean:
mangroves and stingers, crocodiles, dugong,
sunsets and sunrises.
Moons and stars.

Air draped around me like a warm wet blanket.
Feel the seasons
change, and turn.
Sweat through the Build-up.
Dance through the Wet.
Duck as the dragonflies
herald the Dry.

Warm thick soup of the Arafura Sea,
flat as a tack.
Not great for surfing—
—unless there's a cyclone.

Watch the tide surge: in, out, in, out,
a force of life:
relentless. Incessant.

Saltwater girl, me—through and through.
Here in my safe place, where the whole world stops.
And lets me
just
be
me.

▼ ▼ ▼

Dondale Youth Detention Centre.

ELVIS: They ring the last bell and I hear them shuffle in and someone laughs and someone else coughs, someone swears, 'Fuck off, cunt'—

and then the final clang of the big doors, metal on metal, slammin' shut.

The bolt driven home. A bitter and final sound.

Bodie's being shifted to the big house tomorrow. Someone's singin' happy birthday to him. That's what they do in here. On your eighteenth birthday, they shift you across.

He's gone all quiet in his cell. Be shittin' himself. All them stories. Gettin' it up the arse by the big fellas. Havin' the shit punched out of you if you look the wrong way, smell the wrong way, breathe the wrong way. Not knowin' what the right way is, just havin' to learn that, punch by punch. Fist by fist.

Fuck.
Belly turns to jelly just thinkin' about it.

Seven weeks, and I'm outta here. No big house for me, no way.
I'm not getting' it up the arse, ever.
Teach my mind to rise up above here. Float out of my body.
Through the tiny window.
Between the bars.
Onto the hot tin roof.
Rise above the security cameras.
Razor wire.
Spotlights shining twenty-four/seven.
Up beyond the cobwebbed windows of the security tower;
birdshit-stained and concrete-cancered.
Past the Build-up clouds, brewing dense and furious.
Float. Keep floatin'.
Escape.

Mind over matter, that's all it is.
That's all anythin' is.

▼ ▼ ▼

A house in Palmerston.

MADDIE: Wasn't gonna have sex. Not till I was eighteen. Didn't want to be a slut, but then—you can't plan everythin', can you?

… so I'm stuck up this rope wall thingy, one of those stupid trainin' courses where they try to make everyone bond through hatin' the instructor equally. Obstacles and pulleys and ropes and fallin' backwards, hopin' the others'll catch me.

My foot gets caught in a rope square and I can't move. Everyone else is finished, and they're all headin' on to the next thing, and I'm just—

Frozen.

Stranded.

Scared.

Think: I'm gonna be up here forever.

And you're the only one who notices:

Head back to the rope wall thingy.

Climb up beside me.

Smile like it's all gonna be okay.

Say: This sucks, eh? Rather be havin' a beer.

And I tell you I'm scared of heights, and you say: Yeah. Me too.

Then you crawl down a bit.

Unhook my foot from where it's twisted in the ropes.

Come back up. Look me in the eyes.

And I can see in your eyes that you're somethin' special. Somethin' different.

Kind. They're kind eyes.

I'm doin' this with you, you say. Just one foot after the other.

We're doin' this together, okay?

And we do. Together.

And after—when you say: How's about that beer then? I sit in your car at the bottle-o and watch you hand over the money, and I feel like a grown-up for the first time ever. Like you're special, and you picked me, so maybe that means you think I'm special, too.

And that lets me imagine that maybe I am. Special.

Never felt special. Just always felt—
ordinary.
Below ordinary, sometimes.

You get told somethin' long enough, you start to believe it's real.

▼ ▼ ▼

Shady Beach, Yirrkala.

ELVIS: Rosie?
ROSIE: Jesus!
ELVIS: Sorry, I—
ROSIE: What the …?
What're you doing here?
… I thought you were—
ELVIS: I'm out.

Beat.

ROSIE: Right.

Beat.

ELVIS: Thanks for the visits, anyway.
ROSIE: Oh, shove it up your arse.
ELVIS: You coulda come.
ROSIE: I said I wasn't gonna—
ELVIS: You still coulda—
ROSIE: —shift my entire life around to—
ELVIS: —come out to—
ROSIE: —accommodate your screw-ups.

Beat.

ELVIS: 'Shift your life around'? You didn't even come once, Rosie!
ROSIE: I had my Year Twelve!
ELVIS: It's not exactly shiftin' your whole life around to get from your school to there. What is it? Twenty ks? That plus the visit woulda taken you two hours of your life, if that!
ROSIE: Nanna got sick. I had to come back here.
ELVIS: Well, you made a choice then, didn't ya? Her over me. Year Twelve over me.

Coulda written at least. Dumping me for three months without a word.

ROSIE: I meant to write, I just—

ELVIS: Nah. It's lame, is what it is.

ROSIE: Right. Well, I got that message now. Thanks for delivering.

▼ ▼ ▼

MADDIE: The first time, I seriously think I'm gonna die. I mean, that thing's *big*, know what I mean? It's like—how the hell do you get that thing inside here?

And it hurts like hell. And the blood, and the—

I ask my mates: you ever done this? Thalia's the only one who has, and she says sounds like his is bigger than the average. I didn't even know they came in different sizes; I thought they were a 'one size fits all' kinda deal.

But she says no, dicks are different sizes and so are moonies.

You're shitting me, I say. What; so your vag is bigger than mine?

Who're you callin' slack, she says?

And we piss ourselves laughin', and then they ask for more details.

Second time we do it, it doesn't hurt so much and he kind of—he—well, y'know—he kind of—

—he—

—I mean, he—he goes down there. With his tongue. Know what I mean? And I am just: 'Godgodgodgod*ohmygod!*'

I'm not even religious, it just comes out of me. Speakin' in tongues, like my folks. And I—

—I'm just freakin'—

—paralysed. I'm paralysed, and—

Christ. I want more, is all I can say.

So we're kind of a couple now, I guess. Him 'n' me. Me 'n' him. We go places in his car, hang out at the quarry. He gets himself a GoPro off eBay, and keeps it fused to his hip, shootin' everythin' in sight. He's saving up for a big camera, a proper camera. Gonna to move to Sydney and make films.

I know he likes me, coz he laughs a lot when we're together.

I've never made anyone laugh like that before.
Feels good, makin' someone laugh.
Like flyin', on the inside.

▼ ▼ ▼

ROSIE: Why're you here, Elvis?
ELVIS: I come here to dump you.
ROSIE: You drove fifteen hours to dump me?
ELVIS: I wanted to do it face to face.
ROSIE: … Well, that's …
ELVIS: Bettern' doin' it by text.
ROSIE: Yep. Yep, it is.
So—that's it? I'm dumped?
ELVIS: Yep.
ROSIE: Okay. Well—thanks for not doing it by text, and thanks for making the effort to come all this way.
ELVIS: You're welcome.

Beat.

You're worth it, Rosie. Don't let anyone tell ya any different.
ROSIE: So … we're just mates now?
ELVIS: Fuck no. My mate's gotta be loyal.

Beat.

ROSIE: Right then.

Beat.

How'd you get here?
ELVIS: Borrowed a car.
ROSIE: You borrowed one, or you 'borrowed' one.

The latter.

Shit, Elvis. Don't you ever learn?
ELVIS: It's called 'sharin' resources'.
ROSIE: It's called evo-bloody-lution.
ELVIS: It's the last time, promise. But I had to dump you in person. Rude, otherwise. I'll put it back. Even wash it for 'em. Could do with a wash.

ROSIE: Well, by now they've probably reported it, so …

ELVIS: It's an old troopy, been sittin' out there for weeks. Batshit all over it. They won't even miss it. Plus, I swapped the plates.

ROSIE: Well, that is evolution. Did you learn that inside?

ELVIS: I learned a lotta things.

ROSIE: I'm sorry, Elvis. I had so much pressure. My nanna—

ELVIS: *You* were under pressure? Well, fuck me ragged. Were you gettin' shoved up against a wall with a—?

ROSIE: I had stuff going down too. I've had a shitload to deal with. Not that you'd know anything about that, because you never bloody ask!

ELVIS: Woah. Settle. I'm askin' now then. You okay?

Beat.

Look. I'm gonna say something, then I'm gonna go.

Beat.

I'm changed, Rosie. Took a long, hard look at meself in there. Made a deal with meself. That's it. Straight and narrow from now on. Gonna do one of them anger management courses. Keep meself in check.

ROSIE: Okay. Well, that's great to hear. Very responsible of you.

ELVIS: Yeah.

Beat.

It's part of the parole. Along with the curfew.

Beat.

Well, I done what I come for.

ROSIE: You going back then?

ELVIS: Yep.

ROSIE: What's that?

ELVIS: Whadd'ya reckon?

ROSIE: Bush or hydro?

ELVIS: Bush.

Beat.

Want some?

Beat.

Call it a break-up joint …

▼ ▼ ▼

MADDIE: 'The test is designed to read HCG levels, which is the amount of human chorio / cherios / chorionoc …' What? Speak bloody English, dickheads. Blah blah blah blah—ah, here we go. 'You may notice a coloured solution movin' across the test strip. You need to wait ten minutes to confirm the result.'

It says five on the packet. That's why I bought this one.

'If only one coloured line appears as the control line, the test is negative and you can assume you are not pregnant. If two coloured lines appear, the test is positive and you can assume you are pregnant.' Assume? The bloody kit cost me twenty bucks. You'd wanna do more than assume.

'Even if the lines are very light in colour, you can still assume you are pregnant.'

One Line equals Not Pregnant. Two Lines equals Pregnant.

One line One line One line

Two.

Two lines.

… I'm …

fuck.

▼ ▼ ▼

ELVIS: Whatcha doin' out here anyway?
ROSIE: Watching.
ELVIS: What?
ROSIE: The ocean.
ELVIS: Why?
ROSIE: … Just … listening.
ELVIS: Does it talk to ya?
ROSIE: It sings.

ELVIS: Sings?
ROSIE: Yeah.
ELVIS: Bloody blackfellas.
ROSIE: You can't hear it?
ELVIS: Nah.
ROSIE: Maybe you should shut up for a bit then.

Beat.

ELVIS: Nah. Too hard.

Beat.

So what's up?
ROSIE: Had a fight with my dad.
ELVIS: Ah.
ROSIE: He wants me to go back to school to give a speech.
ELVIS: What for?
ROSIE: I got dux, and the school's askin' me to—
ELVIS: Dux?
ROSIE: Yeah. And the school wants me to—
ELVIS: You got dux?
ROSIE: Yeah.
ELVIS: You're shittin' me! Rosie, that's awesome! Dux of the school! A blackfella!
ROSIE: What the fuck?
ELVIS: … I just meant …
ROSIE: I know what you meant.
ELVIS: I meant you're the first one ever and you oughta be proud.
ROSIE: First one for that school, maybe. Not the first one in the whole world.
ELVIS: Whatever.
ROSIE: It's not 'whatever', Elvis. That's the whole point. It's like I now have to be the bloody representative for every Aboriginal person who's ever entered an academic institution. Part of me wonders if they made me dux just coz I'm black.
ELVIS: Ah, bullshit Rosie. You topped that school all the way through. You worked your arse off. Night after night. All weekend. All holidays. 'Elvis, test me on my History. Test me on my Maths.' Well, *that* was a riveting time of my life, I'll give ya that.

ROSIE: I did that coz I wanted to. I don't give a shit about their bloody dux.

ELVIS: Well tell them to take it back.

ROSIE: You can't give dux back, you dickhead.

I just … I don't wanna make a speech. Parading me around like a prize chook.

Talk about fucken shame.

Beat.

Sorry, I'm just—

Beat.

You got any more of that shit?

ELVIS: … here we go …

ROSIE: What happened to the straight and narrow?

ELVIS: This is medicinal. Part of the anger management.

ROSIE: … that'd be the self-prescribed part …?

ELVIS: Now you're gettin' it.

Always were a sixpack ahead of the carton, you were. Dux.

ROSIE: Oh, get fucked.

ELVIS: Duxduxduxduxdux.

▼ ▼ ▼

MADDIE: I google it. Try everythin': papaya, vitamin C, cinnamon, goji berries, parsley. Straighten out a coathanger, but Jesus Christ, can't get it past the first bit, hurts like hell.

Think about rollin' meself down the stairs, but I hate pain.

Bathtub full of hot hot water. Sit in it. Drink gin, like in the old movies.

Nothin'.

Whole pack of laxatives.

… Won't describe that one …

Run out of things to try. Nothing I do kills it. Feels like if it's gone through all that and still hasn't given up, then it's probably stayin'.

Too scared to tell him. Scared he'll dump me. He's the best thing that ever happened to me; I don't wanna lose him. Not over this.

Have to get rid of it.
Need parental permission when you're my age.

... How'm I gonna get that ...?

▼ ▼ ▼

ROSIE: How is she?
ELVIS: Mum?
She's—
she's—
she's—

Beat.

When I get out of juvie, she picks me up and asks me where I want to go. Do I wanna go for a feed, or should she pick up some beers, or—?
And I just want to go straight home, y'know? Just—
—home.
Hadn't been to the new home yet. Knew it was a bit smaller, they'd had to get a Housing Commission, so—
We pull up outside, and it's this—
—concrete box. Next to a whole heapa other concrete boxes.
No yard out the front, even. Just—
—cement.
Weeds growin' up through the cracks of it. Broken bottles, cans, dogshit spread across the front like a putrid fucken welcome mat. Bins not even out on the street; just sittin' there overflowin' as if someone's gonna come along and magic them empty.
I used to look after the old house, y'know? I mean, it was never gonna be a palace, but—it was never a tip, neither.
I'd only been in three months. And this place was already just—
filthy.

And I know it's been a tough time for them, I know that. But if you don't take pride in yourself, then—
Well, ya got nothin', ey?

And I remember when you first brung me out here to meet your mob. Your dad's growin' tomatoes in the front yard. All them things in pots: basil, and ginger, and lemongrass and chillies. Waterin' them every day from an old paint tin, holes hammered into the arse of it. Seeds and seedlings strugglin' through the red sandy dirt.

Then one day there's this small plant with flowers, remember? The first tomato flowers—and your dad's so excited, takin' me on a tour of his tiny little nuggets of hope. And I ask him how he makes that soil produce anythin'; it was like sand. Rough as guts.

And he tells me, every year a third of the seeds make it through. And then of that third, a third of the plants bear fruit that makes it to bein' ripe. And he says that a third of a third is better than nothing.

And I remember thinking he was some kind of idiot. I could never settle for a third of a third. What's the point? I want a hundred percent, every fucking time.

▼▼▼

MADDIE: Tell Mum and Dad. Shit hits the fan. They're Christians. They don't like sluts. Don't like murder much, either. And that's what they're callin' it.

Run away to Nanna's. She takes me in.
Says they're under pressure, need some space.

Nanna's great. Feeds me up. Tell her I need to go down south. Get rid of it. She says she'll help if that's what I want to do. Pay the airfare. Come with me for support. Tells me to think about it for a bit, though. It's a big decision. Life is precious. Describes its growin' soul, already formin'. Its little heart beat-beatin' away.

I google it up. Tell her it's not even an inch long. The size of a raspberry. The size of a Mintie, without the wrapper. No features even, just a head and a blob for a body. It's nothing. Not even human yet.

It's still a person, she says. Suggests adoptin' it out.

That's not gonna happen. Carry somethin' round in my belly for nine months just to give it to someone else? Bugger that for a joke.

Feel my belly growin'. Tits swellin'. Need to piss all the time.

Vomit nine a.m. on the dot, every morning.
And ten.
And eleven.

… she still doesn't book the airfares …

▼ ▼ ▼

ELVIS: How's your nanna?
ROSIE: She—she—she's—
ELVIS: Oh, shit. Rosie. I'm sorry.
ROSIE: I just—
She got sick, and I came back here. Sat with her a bit.
Thought she seemed okay. Thought she was gonna last a bit longer, anyway. And she told me to go back, y'know? Told me to go back to school, to finish my studies, if that's what I wanted.
So I did. I went back. Put my English exam before my nanna's last days.
Missed the chance to—
—say goodbye. Never gonna see her again.

Still can't—still can't believe I did that.
I never asked her the stories, never learned the songs.
Too busy with my own shit.
ELVIS: Well, like you said, you had Year Twelve, and—
ROSIE: Nah, it's—
Lame. I got my priorities all screwed up. Startin' to believe my own publicity.
They're just so—proud of me. The school's one thing, but the family's somethin' else. Dad deadset did a three-day ceremony when I got uni preselection; and you've got no idea how—
ELVIS: Hang on, just—
—back up a bit. Preselection?
ROSIE: Yeah. I got into uni.
ELVIS: Uni? You're going to—Freakin' eh! Of course you are! Rosie, that's awesome! We can get that place together, and I'll get a job, and—
ROSIE: Not in Darwin. Down south.

ELVIS: … down …?

ROSIE: South. They don't offer medicine up here.

ELVIS: Medicine? You've never talked about doing—

ROSIE: Yeah, but I got into Sydney Uni. Do you know how hard that is to—

ELVIS: You hate Sydney! You came back from that excursion early, remember? Said there was too much concrete, and you never once saw the stars. Plus it was full of traffic, and it took you two hours to get anywhere.

You're gonna do Law, remember? In Darwin. We're gonna set up a—

—a place together, and we're gonna—

ROSIE: Yes, but I got preselection for Medicine, and Dad—

Dad wants me—

He wants me to—

ELVIS: All you ever talked about was Law!

ROSIE: This isn't just about me, Elvis. It's a huge opportunity for this community. We need a proper clinic up here. I could bring all that learning back. Do it Yolngu way, but combine it with western ways.

ELVIS: No way, Rosie. That's crazy. That was never the plan.

ROSIE: Plans change, Elvis.

ELVIS: … tellin' me they do …

▼ ▼ ▼

MADDIE: Twelve weeks, and this time she's done the googlin'. Nanna on google, how's that for progress? Shows me the pictures: how it's got its own little legs and arms. Tiny scrunched fingers 'n' toes.

Not real bones yet—just cartilage—but still; the perfect shape of its ribs.

The see-through of its ears. A face all of its own.

Two inches long, she says. The size of a lime.

A miracle, she says. Life is a miracle. Then why doesn't mine feel like that? Feels like plenty of things, but a miracle's not one of 'em.

Start to feel this thing deep in me, like—fear, or—

—terror.

Is this it?

Really?
A mother?
Me? A mother?
Mothers are forever, aren't they?
Not what I wanted to do.
Not sure what I did want to do, but this wasn't in the top ten.

Nanna says I need to think about where I'm gonna live, if I'm gonna have it. Says her place is too small for a baby.

Scared. So scared. Can't do this alone.
Can't go down south without money.
Think about robbin' a bank. Money fixes everythin', doesn't it?

I wouldn't know. I never had any.

Stuck. Don't know what to do.

▼ ▼ ▼

ELVIS: How long's the course?
ROSIE: Seven years.
ELVIS: What the fuck? You'll be twenty-five! Life's practically over by then!
ROSIE: This is a window of possibility for my mob. And I've got the capacity to—
ELVIS: Climb through the fucking window?
ROSIE: Yeah. Okay. Whatever. If you're gonna be an arsehole, then—
ELVIS: Oh, come *on*, Rosie! It's your life, not theirs. They've had theirs.
ROSIE: Back *off*, Elvis. I don't need your bloody lecture as well, okay?

Beat.

ELVIS: Right. Okay. Well, sounds like you've decided, then. So what're we doin' still flappin' our lips? Go pack your bloody bags and make Daddy happy.
ROSIE: Don't be a dick.
ELVIS: It's you who's bein' the dick. Jesus, Rosie. What do *you* bloody want?

Beat.

ROSIE: I—

I—

I—

—wanna stay here. Just for a bit. On Country.

For a month. Six months. A year, maybe.

Listen to the ocean. Think.

Just—

—be.

Beat.

I'm so tired.

Beat.

Dad says there's time for that later. Says after the study I can stay here, but—feels like everyone wants a piece of me. Everyone knows how I should do it different. Better. Even you, apparently.

ELVIS: … what would your Nanna say …?

ROSIE: She'd—

Beat.

—she'd—

—tap my heart with her little skinny finger, and say, 'This, girl. Listen to this. It's tryin' to tell you somethin'.'

She was the one who really got me. Got who I was. But now—?

Feels like my life's been decided for me.

Feel like I'm on a runaway train.

Feels like it's too late to stop it.

▼ ▼ ▼

MADDIE: But then—I dunno. Something shifts. In my brain. Them hormones, maybe. I wake up and think: Why not have it? I'd be alright. I'd be okay at it, at being a mum. Make a little home. Have a little bub. I could do that.

… couldn't I …?

Plenty of people do it. Total dickheads do it, and the kids still turn out okay. Mostly.

So I start to test it out, inside my head. Let the pictures sit in there and swim around:

Me pushin' it in a pram.
Me makin' it the perfect one-year-old birthday cake.
Me 'n' it splashin' around in a paddle pool, laughin'.

And it starts to get real, inside my head.
The thought of havin' somethin' that's mine.
… just …
mine.

Then the pictures start to include you. You'd be great at bein' a dad, Conor. You'd be—

—kind. A kind dad.

So in my head I see you 'n' me at the beach with the baby. Two babies.

Maybe even three. Kids. A family. A proper one.

What's wrong with wantin' that?

And by the end of that week it's all locked in there like a home movie.

Solid in my head, like it's already real.

▼ ▼ ▼

ELVIS: Come on, let's go for a spin. Get some perspective.

ROSIE: In a stolen car? Are you shitting me? My dad'll kill you if he finds you here.

ELVIS: Why? Me 'n' your old man get along. Did last time we—

ROSIE: He doesn't want to see you. Doesn't want me to—

ELVIS: What, just coza one little—?

ROSIE: You've got a criminal record, Elvis.

ELVIS: So he's wiped me, has he? Just coza that?

ROSIE: They've all wiped you.

ELVIS: Well, fuck me, have they never done anything wrong? Your whole family perfect then?

ROSIE: Well, I'm pretty sure none of 'em went around stealing cars and ramming ambulance stations.

Beat.

ELVIS: Is that why they're making you go down south? To get you away from me?

Beat.

That's it, isn't it? Fuck, I could—

ROSIE: Not everything's about you, Elvis.

ELVIS: No, but I bet that is.

Beat.

And you know what? Maybe it's for the best. Ever since I went in, you've been—

ROSIE: Look, I'm sorry for what happened, but—

ELVIS: I had nothin' in there. No-one. And I was—
—scared. So fucking scared. Coulda done with a friend.

ROSIE: I couldn't come, Elvis, I … needed a break.

ELVIS: A break.

ROSIE: Yes. A break.

ELVIS: From me.

ROSIE: Yes. From you.

ELVIS: Why? I'm still the same person! I just got a run of bad luck!

ROSIE: It's not about luck.
It's about—
—it's about—
—it's the choices you make.

Beat.

ELVIS: Some people get better choices to choose from.

▼ ▼ ▼

MADDIE: So I head to the Palmerston CMax. You're not expectin' to see me there, so you know straight away somethin's up. Say somethin' to your mate.
Head towards me: Whassup?
I say we need to find somewhere to chat. Somewhere quiet.
You say: nah, this'll have to do. Film starts in five.
So I tell you, there in the foyer of the Palmerston CMax.
Tell you we're gonna—
—you 'n' me, we're gonna—
—a family, I say. We're gonna be a family.

You go all white. Wasn't the plan, you say.

Wasn't the plan? I say. What was the plan, if you don't mind me askin'?

You gotta get rid of it, you say. I'll pay. You can use my camera money. Okay?

I don't answer.

Okay?

But I've decided. I'm havin' it. And I tell you that if you don't have the balls to see through what you started, then I'll find someone else. A good bloke. A responsible bloke. Someone with the guts to be a dad. Someone I can have more kids with, and make a family.

… and I can see that gets to you …

So we head off for donuts and Coke, and talk about:

What.

When.

How.

I take your hand as we talk, and for the first time ever, you don't pull it away. And for a second I can feel your whole life restin' in mine

and mine in yours.

And it feels—

—safe.

▼ ▼ ▼

ELVIS: Okay. Well.

ROSIE: You going?

ELVIS: Yeah. Not gonna stay here and get spoken to like I'm some fucken child, that's for sure

Beat.

ROSIE: Sorry, Elvis.

ELVIS: It's okay. Things change, and I get that. But I do want to say: I been in court a fair bit—and most of them are ugly cunts. But you? You'd look great in one of them wigs, struttin' around, doin' that—

ROSIE: Shut *up*, Elvis!

Beat.

Dickhead.

ELVIS: Wish we were—

—wish we could—

—go back in time or something. Go back to—

Beat.

We were fucken deadly together, Rosie. Remember that time I broke you out of the boarding house? And we sat in the gutter, outside in the street, and we—talked. All night. And the stars, and the night, and the—sunrise.

You know what I remember most?

ROSIE: What?

ELVIS: Your smell. Like—

—possibility. You smelled like possibility.

I loved that night. Wish we could have that all over again. Just sittin', and talkin', and—

Beat.

Let's go for a drive.

ROSIE: Where to?

ELVIS: Anywhere. Just—

Beat.

What's tonight?

ROSIE: Friday.

ELVIS: Ha! We could—

ROSIE: No way!

ELVIS: Come on!

ROSIE: How you gonna get in, Elvis? You gonna use bolt cutters again?

ELVIS: Nup. I got a licence.

ROSIE: You're seventeen.

ELVIS: Didn't say it was my licence.

ROSIE: … that's Conor's …

ELVIS: Yup. Me 'n him always were peas in a pod.

Come on. Let's go have ourselves a bit of fun.

Fucken karaoke! Yay!

▼ ▼ ▼

MADDIE: I start to show, and the shit hits the fan at school. Some of the blokes call me a slut as I walk past. Couple of them try it on me. I guess they figure: once a slut, always a slut. The girls pretend to give a shit, some of 'em—but you can see they're either thinkin': thank Christ that's not me, or else they got that superior judgment thing happenin' where they're suddenly better'n me in every single freakin' way. My mates are there, mostly, but—

Well; you're on your own in the end with shit like this, aren't you?

So I stop going to school. It's not set up for people like me.
Move into Conor's place with his brother Elvis.
Cow of a mother, but she's never there, so—
Elvis is pretty cool—helps me paint up the bedroom, gets us a cot from the op shop; scores a high chair and a giant panda bear from the pre-cyclone clean-up.
Hoses the bear off a bit. Good as new.
Reckons he's gonna be the best uncle in the whole world.

He probably will be, too.

▼ ▼ ▼

The Arnhem Club, Nhulunbuy. ROSIE *is at the mic.*

ROSIE: [*singing*] I got one foot on the platform
The other on a train
And I'm goin' back to New Orleans
To swing …

ELVIS: *Go, Rosie!*

ROSIE: [*singing*] … that ball …

ELVIS: *Go, girl!*

ROSIE: [*singing*] … and chain.
Yeah, there is a house in New Orleans
They call the …

ELVIS: *Cut sick, Rosie!*

ROSIE: [*singing*] … Rising Sun, and it's been the ruin …

ELVIS: *You're deadly!*

ROSIE: [*singing*] … of many a poor girl …

ELVIS: *Whoooot!*
ROSIE: [*singing*] … and God, I know …
ELVIS: *Go you!*
ROSIE: [*singing*] … I'm one.
ELVIS: You sure *are!*

ROSIE *joins* ELVIS.

That was bloody awesome!
ROSIE: Yessss! I am *awesome! I am Jessica fucking Mauboy!*
ELVIS: I'm up!

ELVIS *delivers the song entirely to—and for—*ROSIE. *He's all hip-swivelling, leg-shaking, hair-combing. The full early Elvis:*

[*Singing*] Well Mama, she done told me,
Papa done told me too
'Son, that gal you're foolin' with …

Rosie!

[*Singing*] … She ain't no good for you',
But, that's alright, that's alright,
That's alright now, Mama, anyway you do.

He does an Elvis leg shake, and the crowd goes wild.

[*Singing*] I'm leaving town tomorrow
I'm leaving town for sure
Well, then you won't be bothered with me
Hanging round your door
Well, that's alright, that's alright
That's alright now, Mama, anyway you do.

He strikes a classic Elvis pose, and the crowd goes utterly apeshit.

[*As Elvis*] Well, thank you very much.

Elvis is now leaving the building.

▼ ▼ ▼

MADDIE: Feel like I hardly know you. Try to get you talkin'.
Tell me a story, Conor.
What about? You say.
About when you were little.

So you tell me how one night when your dad was still around, him and your mum didn't come home at all; so you and Elvis are left alone all night. And there's no food in the house. Elvis is only five, and he starts cryin', he's that hungry. So you try to make something outta this bit of milk and custard powder, but the milk's gone off and the custard powder's crawlin' full of bugs. Then you remember one time when you stashed a pack of M&Ms in your jocks drawer. Bit melted, but they're still there—so you tell me how you get out two bowls and two cups and two of your big plates, and you make Elvis a three-course meal.

You explain all the courses to him like you're at a fancy restaurant: the red and orange ones are prawns, and you even make him peel 'em, coz he's never had a real prawn before. And then roast chicken with potatoes—that's the brown and yellow M&Ms. And the green and blue ones are jelly and blueberry ice-cream.

And I think that's the best story in the world, and how I wish I'd had a brother like you. But you don't see it that way: don't want my kid growin' up like that, you say. I got dreams. Gonna direct films. Can't do that with a kid. Just startin' me own life. Can't give a kid what a kid needs. Not now.

I can feel you gettin' cold feet, so I look you fair in the eyes: lots of people've done it before, I say. And if they can, we can. We just need to learn how to do it; one foot after the other. Together.

I know you're scared, Conor. Me too.
But we can be less scared together.

▼ ▼ ▼

ELVIS: I. Am. Baked.
ROSIE: What's that?
ELVIS: What?

Beat.

Oh.

Beat.

Dunno.

Beat.

Blood. Musta cut meself.

ROSIE: Oh, fuck.

ELVIS: It's not that bad. You got a tissue?

ROSIE: Can't do blood.

ELVIS: Huh? Thought you were gonna be a doctor.

ROSIE: Get it *away!* Jesus.

ELVIS: Hahahahaha. Doctor, my arse.

ROSIE: Ohhhhh. I feel sick.

ELVIS: Seriously? How're you gonna do Medicine if you can't handle blood?

ROSIE: I figure I'll get over it.

ELVIS: Yeah, right.

Beat.

Hey, I got an idea.

ROSIE: Oh-oh. Here's trouble.

ELVIS: Come back with me. To Darwin.

ROSIE: Darwin?

ELVIS: Just for a few days. Come see Maddie. She's *huge*. It's like she's got two of 'em in there.

Beat.

She'd love to see you. She needs someone to talk to—

—and it'd give you a break from your family. Process your options without having everyone stuck in your face.

ROSIE: Can't, Elvis. They'd freak.

ELVIS: Just text them. Say you've gone bush for the weekend.

ROSIE: My phone's back home.

ELVIS: I'll text them then.

Beat.

It's only a thousand ks. Just come for the weekend. Give you all a bit of a circuit breaker. Have you back here by—

ROSIE: Monday.

ELVIS: Monday?

ROSIE: Got basketball training.

ELVIS: We could do that, no worries. Piss it in.

Beat.

ROSIE: … I just don't …
ELVIS: You said you needed a break.
ROSIE: I do, I just …

Beat.

ELVIS: What would your nanna say?

Beat.

ROSIE: She'd—
—she'd—
—she'd—

▼ ▼ ▼

MADDIE: And then you go quiet. Real quiet. Not the same bloke I met up at the rope course.

You're like a shadow. Elvis 'n' me, we try to gee you up, get you out and about, but you're hard to rouse. You stop going to work. Don't wanna go out. Don't wanna eat. Stay in bed all the time. Say you're tired, want to sleep. But you don't. You don't sleep. I can hear you lyin' there at night, not sleepin'.

The sound of someone not sleepin' is the loudest sound in the world.

You won't talk about it, say it's nothin'.
Feel helpless. Don't know what to say or do.
Feel like it's up to me to fix you, but—
—how?

Wish I had a magic wand to make everything better.
But I don't.

No wand.
No magic.
No nothin'.

▼ ▼ ▼

ROSIE *and* ELVIS *drive.*

ROSIE: And we drive: windows down.
Away from this northern cape.
Yirrkala, place of bark and bauxite.
Yirritja and Dhuwa.
Dreams and dust.

Head along Gunyipinya Road. Past the airport.
Dhupuma Road. Past the Telstra tower.
Down Gapuwiyak Road.
Over the Doingy Creek bridge.
Through Bulman.

Away from tiny, hot streets filled with mangy dogs.
Crowded houses full of uncles and aunties, cousin brothers and sisters.
Laughter and singing and bickering and love.

Away from the blue, blue coastline lined with mangroves, mud skippers, dugong, crocodile.
Sunsets and sunrises. Moons and stars.

One thousand ks down the Central Arnhem Highway.
Red dust turns to dirt. Shrubs turn to trees.
Termite mounds rise like ancient ghosts from the land.
And something in me wants to just keep on driving. Forever.

… windows down …

▼▼▼

MADDIE: I start gettin' fat. Like, super-fat. All my clothes are these tight, skimpy little things, and my belly's stickin' out like an oversized basketball. Got no money, so Elvis takes me shopping.

ELVIS: These?

MADDIE: Eww! No! They're super daggy!

ELVIS: So you wanna look like Beyonce when you're popping him out, do you?

MADDIE: Who says it's gonna be a him?
ELVIS: No-one.

Beat.

These?

MADDIE: Well, the style's alright, but they're grey.
ELVIS: Christ, you're hard to please.
MADDIE: Them.
ELVIS: These?
MADDIE: Yeah. Them.
ELVIS: Okay.

ELVIS *rips off the tag and shoves them down his jeans.*

MADDIE: Elvis!
ELVIS: What about this?
MADDIE: Elvis, you can't—
ELVIS: Fuck 'em, Maddie. How much profit d'you think these bastards make? I guarantee you they paid someone two bucks fifty to sit in some sweatshop somewhere and whip this whole table up. That's why we're not in an op shop. I'd never steal from charity. Now do you want this, or not?
MADDIE: Have they got a blue one?
ELVIS: You're not bloody fussy, are you?

Beat.

Not blue, but this red's nice. Matches your eyes.

Nah, gammon!

MADDIE: Dickhead.

Beat.

Yeah, that'll do.

ELVIS *rips the tags off, shoves it down his shirt.*

You're bloody crazy.

ELVIS: Look. Here's five bucks, right? I'll leave that here for them. That'll cover these two tables, no worries. Now let's blow this joint. K-Mart next, eh …? You wanna share the love, or else they—
MADDIE: Oh, Elvis! Look at this.
ELVIS: That's for a girl.
MADDIE: She might be a girl.

ELVIS: She might not be. But even if she is, are you really gonna dress her in that? She'll look like a bloody fruit cake.
MADDIE: Can we get it? Please? It's sweet.
ELVIS: I got no more room. You gotta shove it down your—
MADDIE: Where? Look at my belly, nothin'll fit down th—
ELVIS: —tits. They'll never notice that.
MADDIE: Not with these massive bloody melons they won't, no.
ELVIS: Go on then, I'll cover for you.
That's it.
Now let's go. That bloke's started checking us out.
Just walk normal, like we're …
… you rip the tag off …?

An alarm bell rings.

Bolt, Maddie!
Run!

They run to safety, laughing.

▼ ▼ ▼

ELVIS: … So I got an idea …
ROSIE: Two in one day. That's miraculous.
ELVIS: I'll come with ya. Down south.
ROSIE: And do what?
ELVIS: Get a job. Support you.
ROSIE: Ha.
ELVIS: Marry me.
ROSIE: What the fuck, Elvis.
ELVIS: I'm serious. Marry me. We'll move there together. I'll get a job, support you through uni. You can be a doctor or a lawyer or whatever the fuck you want, I don't give a shit. We'll have babies, and I'll look after them. Then when you're finished studying, you can sort out the world while I look after the kids.
ROSIE: Elvis, you are seriously …
ELVIS: What? I'd be the best dad in the world, and you know it. I got heaps more energy than you. Take them to the park every day. Walk them to school. Fix them dinner. I do a mean spag bog. We'll get a little house somewhere near the ocean, the proper ocean where you

can swim and catch waves. I'll teach 'em how to surf. Teach them no fear of the water. No fear of anythin'.

ROSIE: You don't even know how to surf!

He stops the car.

ELVIS: I mean it. Marry me. We're perfect together. We make each other laugh. We can fight and still sort it out. We never get bored with each other. We keep each other on our toes.

Beat. She's looking at him. Considering the offer.

We're good for each other, Rosie. I lighten you up, and you level me out.

And fuck it, I love you. I've always loved you. That's no secret. Thought you 'n' me would—

Always thought we would—

ROSIE: We're from different worlds, Elvis.

ELVIS: We weren't.

ROSIE: But we are now.

ELVIS: Well, you seem to be makin' sure of that.

Beat.

ROSIE: What about Maddie?

ELVIS: She'll—

Beat.

—she's—

Beat.

They can come too.

ROSIE: Is there not even one small part of your brain that's cemented in reality?

▼ ▼ ▼

MADDIE: Elvis gives me a baby name book, and we go through it together:

ELVIS: Harry?

MADDIE: Nah, sounds like a freakin' ex-prince.

ELVIS: Jude?

MADDIE: Jesus, what books you been readin'?

ELVIS: Adam. I like Adam.

MADDIE: Too Christian.
ELVIS: What about Jarrah?
MADDIE: Jarrah? I never heard that one.
ELVIS: Yeah; like a tree.
MADDIE: I like that one.

Beat.

What if it's a girl?
ELVIS: Alice?
MADDIE: Nah. Too prissy.

Beat.

Beyonce.
ELVIS: No way!

Beat.

How about Ebony? That's a nice name.
MADDIE: Ebony.
ELVIS: Yeah, it's a tree too. Like Jarrah. If they're twins we can start a forest.
MADDIE: Yeah. Okay. That goes on the shortlist.

I test the shortlist out on you, but it's like you're not even present, Conor.

It's like your mind's gone away on holiday, and left your body behind.

And it's lonely, Conor. It's lonely and empty, with you like this.

▼ ▼ ▼

ELVIS: You make your own possibilities, Rosie.
ROSIE: Then why don't you get yourself some ambition? Maybe then I'd—
ELVIS: Marrying you's an ambition. Movin' south's an ambition.
ROSIE: That's mine! Moving south is mine! Get your bloody own.
ELVIS: I just haven't found it yet, what I want. Apart from you. I know I want you.
ROSIE: I'm not a bloody possession! God, I want to shake you! Sometimes I think you're so trapped within that impossibly unrealistic bubble which is your head, that you never stop to look at the total fuck-up you're becoming.

Beat.

Sorry, that was …

ELVIS: … a what …?

ROSIE: No, sorry. That was—

ELVIS: No, that's—

—that's—

—that's—

ROSIE: What're you doing?

ELVIS: Turnin' round

ROSIE: Why?

ELVIS: Because you're giving me the shits. 'Total fuck-up'.

ROSIE: I don't mean that, I just mean—

ELVIS: You used to be my mate, Rosie. Before anything, we were mates.

And you're right. We're from different worlds. And I don't like the world you're heading into. You're turning into one of them. And we were never gonna be that, remember?

So fuck you.

I'm dropping you back home and you can live whatever life everyone else wants you to live, and I'll live mine, and everyone's fucken happy.

Beat.

Total fuck-up.

I'm the one who keeps them all together!

Maddie.

Mum.

Conor, before he—

So take your superior attitude back to your superior freakin' lifestyle, and stick it up your arse.

ROSIE: Don't.

Stop.

Don't go back. I don't wanna go back.

Fuck it, Elvis, I'm—

sorry. I'm just—

—tired. So tired. Feel like I'm being pulled every which way. And sometimes you're part of the pulling.

ELVIS: Me?

ROSIE: Yes, you.

ELVIS: *I* am?

ROSIE: *Yes!*

Beat.

ELVIS: Sorry, I'm—
I thought I was being—
Sorry, Rosie.

ROSIE: No. I'm sorry. You're not a total fuck-up. Sometimes I think you're the realest dude I've ever met, and I know I couldn't've done the last few years without you.

Beat.

ELVIS: What's the percentage?

ROSIE: What?

ELVIS: How much of me is fuck-up and how much awesomest dude?

ROSIE: Fifty-fifty?

ELVIS: Nah.

ROSIE: Forty-sixty?

ELVIS: Now you're talkin'.

Beat.

ROSIE: Come on, I'm sick of thinkin' about it. Turn back around. Let's go to Darwin.

ELVIS: You sure?

ROSIE: Yeah.

ELVIS: Fuck yeah. See? We are *deadly* together.

ROSIE: Yeah. Yes, we are. Deadly.

ELVIS: *Deadly*.

ROSIE and ELVIS [*together*] *Deadly!*

Beat.

ROSIE: Dickhead.

ELVIS: You're a dickhead.

ROSIE: *You're* a dickhead …

▼ ▼ ▼

MADDIE: Four months. Five. Start to feel the baby move about inside me. One day I feel it kick, real hard. So I go to find you, to put your hand on my belly and tell you, looks like we got a footy player in here. Want to make you laugh again, to feel something other than this sadness. But I can't find you.

You're not in bed
not in the toilet
not in the kitchen—

—and that's when the shit hits the fan.

Hear your mum's car pull up.
Gate creak open.
Hear this
scream
scream
screamin'
from underneath the house.
Your mum.
Goin' apeshit.
Nonononono.
Help me.
Help me!
Run down there.
See it.
Surreal.
Run back upstairs, coz I was sure you were in bed.
But you're not.

You're down there.
Underneath the house.
Swingin'
swingin'
swingin' from the rafters
like a warm, wet punchin' bag.

Elvis rings the ambos, but you're already dead. Anyone could see that.

Brown shit runnin' down your legs, dripping onto the floor. Coz that's what happens when your body gives up, Conor. You shit yourself. Nothin' romantic about it. Eyes bulgin' back in your head.

Cheeks all red 'n' puffed up. Tongue hangin' out. Swollen and fat. Already blue.

Your mum's feral. Elvis tries to calm her, but she pushes him off:

'No! Not Conor. Anyone but Conor.'

Claws at you, tries to rip you down. Rips out all her fingernails tryin'.

Ambos arrive and the world moves in slow motion as they:

Cut you down.

Try to restart you with that thingy.

Clear!

Just like in the movies.

They shoot some shit into your mum to calm her down.

Load you into the ambulance. Still pumpin' away at you.

Clear!

Close the doors. Drive you off.

Your mum crumples, and Elvis carries her into bed.

Tucks her in. Like he's the parent, and she's the kid.

I make us both a cuppa tea. In slow motion.

Just like in the movies.

▼ ▼ ▼

ELVIS: I writ you a love song. Got the first bit already, wanna hear it?

ROSIE: Yeah.

He sings:

ELVIS: [*singing*] All the stars up in the sky
Cut them out, cut them fine
Put them inside your eyes
And they'll never ever die …

Beat.

That's the chorus.

ROSIE: It's lovely.

ELVIS: I got it from that Shakespeare cunt we did in Year Ten.

ROSIE: *Romeo and Juliet.*

ELVIS: Yeah, when she says that bit about cutting out all the stars. I saw you inside my head, imagined a tiny pair of scissors and how carefully you'd have to cut around them so's not to nick the tips off of them.

ROSIE: But that's when he's dead.

ELVIS: Yeah, I know, I read it too, remember? I'm just sayin' that's where the idea came from. You don't have to stick to it, you can take an idea and make it something else. That's what ideas are for.

ROSIE: Sing it again.

ELVIS: [*singing*] All the stars in the sky
Let them fall, let them cry
They'll land inside your eyes
Where they'll never ever die.

Beat.

All the choruses are different. I mean, they're similar but not the same words. I hate it when they just repeat a chorus, it's like—I know, I've already heard it. Tell me something I don't know.

ROSIE: You should start a band. Or be a mechanic. You're good at hot-wiring.

ELVIS: That's auto-electrics, not mechanics.

ROSIE: Whatevs.

Beat.

Where you going?

ELVIS: Offroadin'.

ROSIE: Why?

ELVIS: Showin' you something.

ROSIE: What?

ELVIS: Just—wait. Down this bit here, and into—

ROSIE: Oh, my God! That's beautiful!

ELVIS: Isn't it? Come on, let's stretch our legs.

ROSIE: Those water lilies, they're—

Beat.

Shh.

ELVIS: What?

ROSIE: Jabiru. Look. Those blue-green feathers. Like it's glowing.

Beat.

How'd you find this place?

ELVIS: Noticed a heap of birds along the highway on the way in, and figured they must be finding water somewhere here.

ROSIE: God, it's—

—beautiful—

—so—

—peaceful.

They settle into a gentle silence. Give them time, and stillness.

An intimacy builds between them. Maybe that's delicately physicalised.

ROSIE: Imagine living out here.

ELVIS: We could do that.

ROSIE: You reckon?

ELVIS: For sure. I could build us a place, just—on that flat bit, there.

Imagine this as our backyard. No pressure, no humbug.

No-one to tell us what to do.

Just—

—simple. A simple life.

ROSIE: … living the dream …

ELVIS: That's what dreams are for. No point having them if ya don't make them real.

▼ ▼ ▼ ▼ ▼

MADDIE: And that's just the start of the whole world goin' to shit.

Conor's mum locks down in grief.

Her arsehole boss gives her the sack.

The electricity gets cut off coz no-one can pay it.

We get behind in the rent—one week, two—so the landlord sends us threatenin' texts.

Beat.

Then the ambos send us a bill for the transport. Of a corpse.

A twelve-hundred-dollar reminder of a dead son.

Beat.

Tips Conor's mum over the edge, so she tries to top herself as well—

—but all she does is projectile vomit pills and vodka back across the carpet.

… so when the landlord comes round and starts chuckin' our stuff out onto the street, Elvis loses his shit: punches the dude's face into a pulpy mess. Then while the fella's lyin' blood-wet on the floor, Elvis steals his car and goes on a rampage; rammin' the ambulance station again, and again, and again.

That night when the doorbell rings, I already got this feeling. Deep inside my guts, I know. And I stand there, staring at the door. Not openin' it.

But I have to eventually, coz they won't go away.

See them standin' there, flashin' their badges. See the peaks of their hats. The blue of their uniforms. The serious on their faces.

His mum shakin' her head, Nonononono. Not him as well. I can't lose my other son. Looking at me, as if it's my fault. As if I started all this.

And Elvis is just standin' there, ready to go with them.
Like he's known all along this was comin'.
Like he's known for years.
Goes to his mum, gives her a hug. Gives me one too.
Look after each other, okay?
Heads out the door with them, cool as anythin'.

Sometimes I wonder what would've happened if I met him first.
Instead of Conor.

Doesn't do to wonder though, does it?
Life's got its own way of decidin' things for you.

▼ ▼ ▼

ELVIS: Pull in to Katherine. Fuel up.
ROSIE: I'll do it.
ELVIS: Got reception here. Stretch me legs.
Text Maddie: Katherine. Three hours to go.
Blokes at the next car checkin' Rosie out.
'Flash car. Not.'

She keeps filling.
'Blackfella car, is it? All covered in batshit.'

Feel the blood heatin' up in me.
Army jerks. Out on the town:
shiny shoes
shiny teeth
shiny hair.
Smell of bourbon comin' off 'em. Too pissed to stand upright.

Clock Rosie. She shakes her head.
Back off, she's mouthin'. Just back off.
And I try.
Breathe.
Count inside my head, like they taught me.
In-out. One breath.
In-out. Two.

'Nice arse.'
Fuck, I'm gonna …
'Is that black too?'

And that's it.
Fuck you! Fuck you! Racist fucken prick!
Slam him. Hard. One punch he don't see comin'. Out cold.
Other one too pissed to react. Deck him to the concrete.
Head slams down hard. Knee in his chest, pinnin' him down—

ROSIE: Elvis!

ELVIS: My arm keeps—
—poundin'
poundin'
poundin'
fist clenched with a life of its own
slicin' through the air
landin' *bam* in the soft white of his face
again / again / again.
Splittin' his lips, nose, eyeballs

pulp ’n’ mash
teeth in splinters.
Teach him, the fucken—

Someone pullin’ me off.
Rose. It’s Rosie.

ROSIE: You’re on parole!

ELVIS: My fist freezes mid-punch.
Feel Rosie draggin’ me off him.
Pushin’ me into the car.
Grabs my wallet. Goes to pay.
The bloke claws himself up.
Drags his mate to their car.
Heels scrape along concrete.
Folds him in. Drives him off.

Good fucken riddance.

Breathe—in-out, in-out.

Wipe the blood from my fists, down my jeans, across my t-shirt.
Wipe him off me.
Scum.

▼ ▼ ▼

MADDIE: I miss you, Conor. Wonder if that’ll ever stop.
And I’m—I’m sorry, I can’t help but—
—sometimes I feel that if I hadn’t—
—if I hadn’t kept it, then—
—maybe you’d still be here.

Beat.

But I have to keep it now, Conor. Part of you. The only part left.

A part of you that might love me, one day.

Because it has to, doesn’t it? A kid? It has to love you, or else it dies.

Well, it has to need you, anyway.

Need.
Love.
They're different, aren't they?

▼ ▼ ▼

ROSIE: What the hell d'you think you're doing?
ELVIS: He dissed ya.
ROSIE: You're on parole!
ELVIS: He sexually harassed you.
ROSIE: That's not your bloody fight! That's mine!
ELVIS: You're my girl. It's a reflection on—
ROSIE: I'm not 'your girl'. Get that through your thick skull! Jesus, Elvis, you're too aggro. I can't be with you. Goin' off every second. Doing stupid shit like that. Thought you were gonna grow out of it, but clearly that's not the case. What the hell is wrong with you?
ELVIS: Gonna do an anger management course.
ROSIE: Sure you are.
ELVIS: I am. Gonna change.
ROSIE: Well, stop talking about it and just do it!

Actually, know what? Forget it. You're never gonna change. You're never gonna be anythin' but what you are. An angry, fucking idiot.

Here. I'm takin' fifty bucks. I'll pay it back. I'll find my own way home.

She walks off.

ELVIS: Fine then. Good luck with that.
Fuck you.
Fuck you.
Stupid fucken—
Jesus.
Fuck.
Fuck!
Fucken idiot dickhead.
MADDIE: What if I screw it up?
ELVIS: Dickhead dickhead dickhead.
MADDIE: What if I'm the worst mother that's ever been?

ELVIS: Can't you get anything right?
MADDIE: What if I hate it?
ELVIS: Look up.
MADDIE: What if it hates me?
ELVIS: Bloke from the servo.
MADDIE: I think I want it.
ELVIS: Takin' photos.
MADDIE: But how do I know?
ELVIS: And it hits me.
MADDIE: Too late now.
ELVIS: Fuck.
MADDIE: There's no guarantees, are there?
ELVIS: Fucked.
MADDIE: There's no guarantees of anythin'.
ELVIS: I've fucked it.
MADDIE: It's gone very still in there.
ELVIS: I'm gone.
MADDIE: Gone all—
ELVIS: Feel sick.
MADDIE: —weird.
ELVIS: In my stomach.
MADDIE: Don't know what to—
ELVIS: Form a plan: Ditch the car.
MADDIE: Ohhhhhhhhhhhh.
ELVIS: Hitch south.
MADDIE: Pains.
ELVIS: Interstate.
MADDIE: Stabbing.
ELVIS: Until it clears.
MADDIE: … that doesn't feel …
ELVIS: Shit. Parole.
MADDIE: Ooooooooooooooooh.
ELVIS: I can't leave.
MADDIE: Sharp, in my—
ELVIS: I'm gone.
MADDIE: That feels like—
ELVIS: Oh, Christ.

MADDIE: That feels wrong.
ELVIS: I'm gone.
MADDIE: Not supposed to have pains yet.
ELVIS: Ohhhh, God.
MADDIE: Where's Elvis?

She sends a text. ELVIS *'s phone pings.*

Oh, Jesus, it's comin'.
ELVIS: What the fuck?
MADDIE: But it can't, it's not—
ELVIS: You're weeks off yet.
MADDIE: Ooooooooh.

She dials, listens.

No credit.

ELVIS *dials. It goes to message.*

ELVIS: Maddie, hang up. I'll call you ba—

He checks his phone.

Shit. Flat.
Rosie!
MADDIE: Oooooohhhhh.
ELVIS: *Rosie!*
ROSIE: Don't follow me!
ELVIS: Maddie's having it.
MADDIE: Stomach hardens.
ROSIE: Now? But she's—
ELVIS: Something's wrong. Where's your phone?
ROSIE: Back home.
MADDIE: Cramp-crampin'.
ELVIS: Get in.
ROSIE: … Not if you're gonna …
ELVIS: *Get in!*
MADDIE: Pain.
ROSIE: I'm driving.
ELVIS: No, you're—
MADDIE: Sharp.
ROSIE: I'm driving!

MADDIE: Piercin'—
ELVIS: Well hit it!
MADDIE: —my ribs.
ROSIE: Headlights carve their way across the night: Edith Falls.
MADDIE: Twistin'.
ROSIE: Ferguson River.
MADDIE: Stabbin'.
ROSIE: Nitmiluk.
ELVIS: Step on it!
ROSIE: Pine Creek.
MADDIE: Can't breathe.
ROSIE: Hayes Creek.
MADDIE: What's that?
ROSIE: Adelaide River.
MADDIE: Is that—?
ROSIE: Lake Bennet.
MADDIE: That's—
ELVIS: What if she's—?
MADDIE: That's—
ROSIE: Manton Dam.
MADDIE: That's—
ELVIS: … What if she's …?
MADDIE: Blood?
ELVIS: Shoulda been there.
MADDIE: … not supposed to—
ELVIS: Should be helpin'
MADDIE: Not supposed to—
ROSIE: Noonamah.
MADDIE: Everywhere, it's—
ROSIE: Humpty Doo.
MADDIE: —down my thighs.
ROSIE: Bees Creek.
MADDIE: On my feet.
ELVIS: Come *on!*
ROSIE: McMinn's Lagoon.
MADDIE: Blood, clotted.

ROSIE: Fred's Pass.
MADDIE: Spinnin' out.
ROSIE: Coolalinga.
MADDIE: So scared.
ROSIE: Yarrawonga.
MADDIE: Gonna faint.
ELVIS: Left. Here.
MADDIE: The pain, it's—
ELVIS: *Left!*
MADDIE: What's that?
ELVIS: Right.
MADDIE: That's the—
ELVIS: Right here.
MADDIE: Oh, God. That's the—
Nonononono.
ELVIS: Here!
MADDIE: Aaaaarrgghhhhhh.
ELVIS: Pull up here.
MADDIE: Please. Stop.
ELVIS: Sprint inside.
MADDIE: Elvis?
ELVIS: Oh, Jesus.
MADDIE: I'm sorry I'm sorry.
ROSIE: Elvis, there's—
MADDIE: Elvis, stop it.
ROSIE: —blood …
MADDIE: What's happenin'?
ELVIS: I gotcha. It's okay, Maddie, it's—
ROSIE: Can't do blood.
MADDIE: It's not supposed to—
ELVIS: Rosie, get towels!
MADDIE: Hurts.
ROSIE: Gonna puke.
MADDIE: Help me.
ELVIS: *Towels!*
MADDIE: Oooooooooooooooooh.
ROSIE: Can't do blood.

ELVIS: *Now!*
MADDIE: Make it stop!
ELVIS: Maddie, you're—
MADDIE: Elvis? Make it—
ELVIS: Hospital.
ROSIE: Here [*the towels*] …
ELVIS: In the troopy.
ROSIE: She could die.
ELVIS: *Now!*
ROSIE: Call an ambulance.
ELVIS: No.
ROSIE: Too much blood, she's—
ELVIS: Come on, Maddie—
ROSIE: —haemorrhaging—
ELVIS: —in the car.
MADDIE: Oooooooooooooooooh.
ROSIE: Ring an—
ELVIS: *No ambulance!*
MADDIE: Ohhhhh, Jesus.
ROSIE: I'm gonna puke.
ELVIS: Help me.
MADDIE: I don't like it!
ELVIS: In the back.
MADDIE: Oohhhhhhhhhh.
ROSIE: Buckle in.
MADDIE: Jesus *Christ!*
ROSIE: Breathe, Maddie.
ELVIS: Twenty-two ks.
ROSIE: All that blood—
ELVIS: McInnis Circuit.
ROSIE: —pouring out of her.
ELVIS: Driver Avenue.
MADDIE: It's comin' out!
ELVIS: Cut the roundabout.
ROSIE: Gonna puke.
ELVIS: Kirkland Road.
MADDIE: Why's there blood?

ROSIE: Warm.
ELVIS: Wishart.
ROSIE: Wet.
MADDIE: Elvis?
ELVIS: Tivendale.
MADDIE: What's wrong?
ELVIS: Hang on, Maddie.
ROSIE: All over me.
MADDIE: Help me, Elvis!
ELVIS: Onto the highway.
ROSIE: Puke.
ELVIS: Vanderlin Drive.
ROSIE: Can't help it.
MADDIE: Noooooooooo.
ROSIE: Chucking up.
ELVIS: Lee Point Road.
MADDIE: Ohgod ohgod.
ROSIE: Spit it out.
ELVIS: Nearly there.
ROSIE: Chunks of sick.
ELVIS: Red light. Fucken fuck.
MADDIE: *Aaaaarrrggghhhh!*
ELVIS: Bust the light.
ROSIE: Blue/red/blue/red.
ELVIS: Cops!
ROSIE: Siren screams.
ELVIS: *Drive!*
ROSIE: Stop, Elvis!
ELVIS: Get her there.
ROSIE: Let the cops—
ELVIS: No time.
MADDIE: Aaaaaaargh!
ELVIS: Left onto Tambling.
ROSIE: Breathe, Maddie.
ELVIS: Right onto Florey.
ROSIE: In.
ELVIS: Hang on, Maddie.
ROSIE: Out.

MADDIE: I can't, I can't.
ROSIE: Slow down, Elvis!
MADDIE: It's coming!
ROSIE: *Elvis!*

ELVIS: We're here.
Get her out. Into emergency.
Onto a stretcher.
You're okay, Maddie, you're alright.
They wheel her away. Down the hall.
So scared. She's just a kid.
MADDIE: Stay with me!
ELVIS: I can't, Maddie. I—
MADDIE: Please, Elvis!
ELVIS: I'm sorry, Maddie.
MADDIE: Stay—
ELVIS: They've taken her.
Oh, Jesus. She's—
—just a kid.
Look after her, Okay?
ROSIE: Yeah.
ELVIS: Stay here with her.
ROSIE: Yes, I—
ELVIS: Ring the station. As soon as you know. Understand?
Get the hospital to ring the station.
ROSIE: Yes.
ELVIS: Promise me?
ROSIE: I promise.
Cops stride through the sliding doors.
He nods at them.
Then back at me.
ELVIS: Okay, well …
… it's been fun …
ROSIE: Elvis, I—
ELVIS: You only got one life, Rosie. Go hard, okay?
Don't settle for a third of a fucking third.
Promise me?
ROSIE: I—

ELVIS: Promise me!

ROSIE: Yes.
Yes.
I—
—I—
—I promise.

ELVIS: Attagirl.
… and come and fucken *visit* me this time …!

ROSIE: Watch them take him away.
Put the cuffs on.
Tuck his head down to get him in.
Into the back seat.
Just like in the movies.
Sits in there with his head held high.
Proud, even now.
And I know, then.
He's never gonna change.
He'll never be anything but him.
Seventy percent awesome, and thirty percent fuck-up.

Or maybe he's right.
Maybe some people just get better choices to choose from.

▼ ▼ ▼

ELVIS: They ring the last bell in this hot stinkin' cell.
Smell of mildew and piss. Tiny barred window, way up high.
Sound of fear risin' up through the concrete floors.
Clang of the big doors, metal on metal.
The bolt driven home. A bitter and final sound.

Feels like a cyclone buildin' up in here.
All the light bein' sucked out into the vortex.

Dark.
Just the dark left.
Just me 'n' the dark.
Don't like the dark.

Think about Maddie. When I'm outta here, I'll get a job. Save up.

Buy her a little house, somewhere near the ocean. The proper ocean, where you can swim and surf and catch waves. A place where she can feel the sun on her back. Get better. Get over the loss, the—

—grief.

MADDIE: Kind. They're kind eyes.

ELVIS: Help her start again.

MADDIE: Peas in a pod, those two.

ELVIS: Three years. That's not forever.

MADDIE: Go visit him every weekend.

ELVIS: I'm eighteen in August.

MADDIE: He says it helps pass the time.

ELVIS: Six months in here, and then—

—the big house.
Fuck.
Fuck.
Fuck.

Don't think about it.

Teach my mind to rise up above here.
Float out of my body.
Through the tiny window.
Between the bars.
Onto the hot tin roof.
Rise above the security cameras.
Razor wire.
Spotlights shining twenty-four/seven.

Float past everythin' that's ever been and gone.
Past the Wet Season clouds just hangin' there,
full of rain and promise.

Look south, west, north, east.
Find her there, on the edge of her ocean:
Saltwater girl.
Staring out into the Arafura Sea.

ROSIE: Feel the seasons
change and turn.
Sweat through the Build-up.
Dance through the Wet.
Fly with the dragonflies
to herald the Dry.
ELVIS: Mind over matter, that's all it is.
ROSIE: Watch the tide surge: in, out, in, out,
ELVIS: That's all anythin' is.
ROSIE: A force of life:

Boundless.

… Infinite …

THE END

Mary Anne Butler

DIRECTOR FRASER CORFIELD
DRAMATURG JANE FITZGERALD
SET DESIGNER CJ FRASER-BELL
LIGHTING DESIGNER JESSIE DAVIS
SOUND DESIGNER & PRODUCTION MANAGER (DARWIN SEASON) BRAD FAWCETT
SOUND DESIGN MENTOR MATT CUNLIFFE
STAGE MANAGER (DARWIN SEASON) SCOTT GOODING
STAGE AND PRODUCTION MANAGER (SYDNEY SEASON) SORIE BANGURA
CULTURAL CONSULTANT ROSEALEE PEARSON

CAST
MADDIE STEVIE JEAN
ELVIS JOSH MCELROY
ROSIE NYASHA OGDEN

PRODUCTION PREMIERE:
BROWN'S MART THEATRE, DARWIN
22 OCTOBER–2 NOVEMBER 2019

INTRODUCTION

WHILE Australia's unique accent, humour, and social norms have been making their way onto Australian stages since the 1950s, outstanding works driven by teenage characters are still finding their place in our national canon. Michael Gow's *Away* gave us a family drama driven by two teenage characters in 1986, then Nick Enright's *Blackrock* took the dark world of adolescence into the spotlight in 1995, but I would argue it's only in the past decade that complex, sophisticated plays driven and populated by teenage characters have been regularly recognised as works of artistic excellence in their own right in Australia.

Plays such as Lachlan Philpott's *Silent Disco*, Declan Greene's *Moth*, Angela Betzien's *War Crimes*, Rachael Coopes' *Sugarland* and Kate Mulvany's brilliant adaptation of *Jasper Jones* present fiercely Australian characters navigating the complexities of growing up and fitting in. They are not specifically plays for young people. They are outstanding plays that happen to feature young people.

Cusp is the latest addition to this important emerging canon of work. It is a beautifully written drama imbued with the specificity of the Top End, elevating everyday young lives and bringing them into the spotlight with a blend of poetry and disarming honesty. The language, themes and complexities of this play are not specific to a teenage audience—indeed in many instances, it is too confrontational to be suitable for schools. This is a play that gives wider society a window through which to view characters we may otherwise never notice or attempt to understand.

Cusp offers three beautifully drawn teenagers, each wrestling with decisions that will change their lives. It's a play about those thresholds in life that must be crossed in one form or another. Each character is forced to accept a level of responsibility that heralds the arrival of adulthood. *Cusp* is a reflection on moments of reckoning; those times in our lives that leave us older, sadder, wiser. These are the moments that make us the people we become.

In reading this play, it's important to remember these characters never feel sorry for themselves. They should not be wallowing in sadness or indulging painful memories moment by moment. They've grown up with hardship, they know how to hide it. One of the delights of *Cusp* is the wry self-deprecating humour that flows through the scenes offering a counterpoint to the drama that peppers the characters' lives. It's this laughter in the face of adversity that gives colour and depth to the story and maintains the action's momentum. The humour allows us to fall in love with each of these people, and once we love them we are prepared to invest in their story.

Cusp is a daunting proposition for actors because the language only flies if we genuinely feel for the characters, believe in their relationships, see the truth in their turn of phrase. It is one thing to read the words on the page, it is another to bring them to life. The key to unlocking this play is stripping away sentimentality and focusing on truth. How do we truly hide our fears, our dreams, our love and our sadness, and what are those moments that give us away? If the characters wear their heart on their sleeve we'll turn away. That's what we do as Australians. No-one likes a whinger, no matter how potent the hardship behind it.

Cusp deserves to be read, to be studied and to be performed for years to come. It offers a significant snapshot of Australian society at this time in our national history.

Fraser Corfield

Director

CREATIVES AND CAST

MARY ANNE BUTLER
PLAYWRIGHT

Mary Anne Butler's plays have won the Victorian Prize for Literature, Victorian Premier's Literary Award for Drama and two NT Chief Minister's Book of the Year Awards (for *Highway of Lost Hearts*, and *Broken*). She has won five NT Literary Awards for Best Script (2010, 2012, 2014, 2018 and 2019) and twice been nominated for the Nick Enright Award. Mary Anne is a Sidney Myer Creative Fellow, an Arts NT Fellow, a Winston Churchill Fellow, a Regional Arts Fellow and an Asialink Fellow. She holds an MPhil in Creative Writing and an MEd in Arts Education, and is co-Artistic Director of Knock-em-Down Theatre.

FRASER CORFIELD
DIRECTOR

Fraser is a director, dramaturg and the Artistic Director of Australian Theatre for Young People (ATYP), the national youth theatre company. He has over 20 years experience in the development and presentation of theatre with and for young people and has worked in collaboration with leading companies, festivals and venues across Australia and internationally. Fraser has been the Artistic Director of Backbone Youth Arts (Qld), Riverland Youth Theatre (SA) and the Associate Director of La Boite Theatre (Qld). He has spent much of his career involved in commissioning and developing new work. Scripts and productions he has initiated have won most of Australia's performing arts awards including Helpmann, AWGIE, Sydney Theatre and Sidney Myer Awards amongst others. Fraser has directed over 50 productions that have performed across Australia as well as the UK, Japan, Canada, South Africa and the USA.

JANE FITZGERALD
DRAMATURG

Jane is Resident Dramaturg at ATYP. Recent productions for ATYP include *April Aardvark*, *Bathory Begins*, *Intersection 2019: Arrival*, *Charlie Pilgrim*, *Impending Everyone* and *Wonder Fly*. Other recent work includes *Black Cockatoo*, *The Appleton Ladies' Potato Race* (Ensemble), *Lost Boys* (Merrigong), *The Big Dry* (co-production Ensemble/ATYP) and *MRock* (co-production ATYP/STC). Previously Jane has been a literary manager at Ensemble Theatre (shared role). For ATYP Jane has been a mentor/dramaturg on the Fresh Ink writers' program and at the National Studio. For STC she has been literary manager, artistic associate and administrator of the Patrick White Playwrights' Award as well as a dramaturg on the Blueprints new writers' program and on mainstage productions. She has worked as a script reader for the Royal Court, ANPC, Playworks and STC Young Playwrights' Award and has also worked extensively as a mentor with Year 12 students on HSC creative writing projects.

CJ FRASER-BELL
SET DESIGNER

Cj Fraser-Bell is a queer artist and producer working across theatre, visual art, and multi art-form performance practice in Darwin. Cj is the former Director of the Darwin Fringe Festival, was the 2018 Artist in Residence at the NT Library, and has worked in the creation, production and management of arts projects in Darwin for close to a decade. Cj's creative practice is collaborative, cross-disciplinary, informed by place, and creates opportunities for experimentation.

JESSIE DAVIS
LIGHTING DESIGNER

Jessie Davis is a freelance audio and lighting tech, musician and emerging lighting designer. She has been involved in theatre since 2014 and has worked on many shows that have graced the Brown's Mart stage, with the help of mentorships and hands-on experience, she has developed a keen interest in lighting. Some of her design credits include *Neuromantic: A Queer Cabaret* (2019 Melbourne Fringe), *And I'm the Queen of Sheba* (2019 Brown's Mart Shimmer Season), *The Sound of Waiting* (2017 Brown's Mart Shimmer Season), and *Hillbilly Horror* (2016 Brown's Mart Shimmer Season).

BRAD FAWCETT
SOUND DESIGN

Born in South Australia, Brad has been in Darwin on and off for almost 20 years. After studying music and production at Charles Darwin University he has worked in performing and community arts, as well as pursuing his own practice in music. Brad is interested in working with sound to translate sensory and emotional experience. His sound design is concept based and sometimes inspired by the Northern Territory environment. Brad is currently the Production Manager at Brown's Mart Theatre.

MATT CUNLIFFE
SOUND DESIGN MENTOR

Matt Cunliffe is an ARIA award-winning musician, sound engineer, and composer with a wide range of live and studio-based experience. Career highlights to date include more than 50 soundtracks for NT arts companies including Brown's Mart Productions, Darwin Theatre Company, Gary Lang NT Dance Company, Knock-em-Down Theatre, and Tracks Dance.

SCOTT GOODING
STAGE MANAGER (DARWIN PREMIERE)

Scott Gooding has worked in numerous roles in theatre since 1987. He created Vicious Fish Theatre which has produced *360 Positions In A One Night Stand*, *The Belbel Project*, a series of four works by playwright Sergi Belbel, and the *Eric–The One Man Sketch Comedy Show* trilogy that was written by a number of Melbourne independent playwrights. Recent acting credits include *The City They Burned* by Fleur Kilpatrick (Attic Erratic), *Cuckoo* by Jane Miller (15 Minutes From Anywhere), *Agni–Lit By Fire* by Robert Reid (Apollon Studios) *Cock* by Mike Bartlett (15 Minutes From Anywhere), and *Robert In Crisis*, self written and performed at La Mama, Darwin Fringe and Perth Fringe World. Since moving to Darwin he has stage managed *And I'm The Queen Of Sheba* (Brown's Mart Theatre).

SORIE BANGURA
STAGE AND PRODUCTION MANAGER (SYDNEY PREMIERE)

Sorie has been with ATYP since 2002, attending many workshops in the process and eventually making the shift to assisting and teaching. As a stage manager Sorie has worked on ATYP productions *Follow Me Home* (2019), Intersection 2019: *Arrival*, *Charlie Pilgrim (Or a Beginners Guide to Time Travel)* (2018), *Dignity of Risk* (2017), *Fight With all Your Might the Zombies of Tonight* (2016), *War Crimes* (2015), *Rainbows Ending* (2011), *Click* (2011), and for the NSW State Public Schools Arts Unit with *The Grandfathers* (2012), *The Miracle* (2012), *We Lost Elijah* (2013), *What Are They Like* (2013), *Cyberbile* (2014), and *DNA* (2015) along with OnStage, Writers OnStage and the NSW State Drama Festival since 2012, and *Pronoun* (2015) with Bittersweet Productions. He was production assistant on *Spring Awakening*—The Musical for ATYP (2016). Sorie has also worked as an actor in several productions including the 2004 Sydney Festival and the 2006 Adelaide Fringe Festival. He has also appeared onscreen in *All Saints* and the short film Secrets of Seduction.

ROSEALEE PEARSON
CULTURAL CONSULTANT

Rosealee is a Yolngu woman from Yirrkala in North East Arnhem Land. In 2005 she graduated From NAISDA Dance College. Rosealee has worked across many disciplines as a dancer, actor, tour manager, event co-ordinator, stage manager, choreographer and cultural consultant. She has toured both nationally and internationally. She has worked with Insite Arts, Compagnia TPO, Performing Lines, Djuki Mala (Chooky Dancers), Curious Works, ATYP, Kaldor Public Arts Project, Moogahlin Performing Arts Inc, Artback NT, Belvoir St. Theatre, Urban Theatre Projects, Shaktidharan Sivanathan, Performance Space, Bell Shakespeare Company, Boomerang Festival, Sydney Festival. After a five-year hiatus, Rosealee has decided to give the arts another go, but only for Maryanne, cause let's be honest, she's a dead set legend.

STEVIE JEAN
MADDIE

Stevie is an emerging actress and singer-songwriter from the Northern Territory. At age 20 she has performed in multiple professional theatre productions, including Brown's Mart Theatre's *Mr Takahashi and Other Falling Secrets* (2017) and *A Smoke Social* (2018). She has also toured nationally as a musician and supported Montaigne on her *Complex* Album Tour in November 2019.

JOSH MCELROY
ELVIS

Josh is an emerging actor who began his working life with bAKEHOUSE Theatre Company. Credits with bAKEHOUSE include *Visiting Hours* (VIVID 2016), *Two Chairs* (2013), *A Land Beyond The River* (2012) and *The Life Of Galileo* (2009). In 2015 he premiered the role of Mike in the national tour of *Connected*, a new musical by Craig Christie. In 2016 he appeared in ATYP's *Spring Awakening*—The Musical and *Low Level Panic* (Old Fitz). Productions in 2017 include *Osama The Hero* (Kings Cross Theatre), *Blackrock*, *Oedipus Doesn't Live Here Anymore* (ATYP, GLUG nomination, Most Outstanding Performance By A Newcomer), *One Flew Over The Cuckoo's Nest* (Sport For Jove), *DNA* (Sydney Fringe Festival), and *Asylum* (Brave New Word). In 2018 he appeared in the *Visiting Hours* return season, *A Town Named Warboy* (ATYP national tour), and *Ned: The Musical* (New Theatre). Most recently he appeared in *Alice In Slasherland* (Old Fitz), *Mercury Fur* (Kings Cross Theatre) and appeared in the ABC/SKYUK series *Frayed*.

NYASHA OGDEN
ROSIE

Nyasha is a 16-year-old Larrakia girl, born and bred in Darwin. She began drama with Corrugated Iron Youth Arts at the age of 12 and continues to be actively involved with them as a student and a tutor. Her stage experiences include *Mr Takahashi and Other Falling Secrets*, *Unbroken Land*, and *Animal Farm*. Her most recent role was the leading character in *Lord of the Flies*. Nyasha's film work includes the short film *Rite of Passage* (Darwin International Film Festival).